DOGS

DOGS

Vida Adamoli

SMITHMARK

First published in the United States in 1992
by SMITHMARK Publishers Inc.,
16 East 32nd Street, New York, NY 10016

in association with Reed Consumer Books
a division of Reed International Books Limited

Copyright © 1992 Reed International Books Limited

Reprinted 1992

ISBN 0-8317-2187-1

SMITHMARK books are available for bulk purchase for sales
promotion and premium use. For details write or telephone
the Manager of Special Sales, SMITHMARK Publishers Inc.,
16 East 32nd Street, New York, NY 10016; (212) 532-6600.

Printed in China

CONTENTS

INTRODUCTION

For over 10,000 years human and dog have enjoyed a unique and very special relationship. During this long and fruitful partnership the dog has responded to care, protection and love by performing many vital tasks. Dogs will guard our property, herd our livestock, join our hunts, work alongside our police and guide our blind.

Dogs make lively and at times entertaining pets, and are remarkably loyal companions. In 1923 an American mongrel called Bobbie lost his master while they were on holiday in Indiana. Six months later, thin and exhausted, he turned up at home in Oregon. He had travelled over 5000 miles to be reunited with the master he adored.

Hardly a week goes by without some act of canine courage or devotion being publicized. Dogs come to our rescue when we're in trouble, alert us to potential disasters and protect us from attack. From wily mongrels to aristocratic show champions, pampered pets to highly trained working dogs, these animals continue to enrich our lives. This book is a tribute to the creature that has truly earned its title as Human's Best Friend.

THE DOG AS A PET

All puppies seem irresistible but it's very important when choosing a pet to imagine it fully grown. Dogs like exercise and the larger breeds need up to 10 miles each day. A big dog can also eat you out of house and home! Small breeds are better suited to flat life, while spaniels, collies and most of the hounds are famous for getting on well with children.
Whether obtained from a breeder, pet shop, dogs' home or a friend, a young dog will soon adapt to new surroundings.

For thousands of years the dog and cat have enjoyed the unrestricted freedom of the human home, equally benefiting from care and affection. Outside this domestic alliance, however, a natural enmity remains, as anyone who has witnessed a spitting, clawing, barking confrontation can confirm.

The canine instinct on meeting a cat is to bound over and give it a thorough sniffing. This causes the cat to bristle defensively, arch its back and possibly lash out. Cats are intimidated by the sheer size of dogs, and territorial jealousy can be an added problem.

Some dogs are incorrigible cat-chasers, setting off in hot pursuit of every feline that crosses their path. Kittens and puppies who have been carefully introduced, however, almost always get on well. It's remarkable how quickly these supposed enemies become playmates, often even sharing the same basket.

Dogs need to run both for play and exercise, and most don't get enough opportunity. Lack of exercise affects not only weight, muscle tone and respiratory efficiency, it also affects a dog's mood. Animals that are cooped up for long periods can become neurotic and lose that sharp canine interest in the world around them.

Dogs love chasing and being chased, happily switching roles many times in the course of a game. A tearing run with an energetic companion is equally savoured.

When let off the lead many dogs put on an elaborate display of leaping, twisting, jumping and wild zigzagging runs. This is both a way of letting off steam and a canine invitation to join in the fun.

A heavy snowfall transforms a dog's everyday world into a strange and magical place. Familiar points of reference vanish, sounds are mysteriously muffled and scent trails all but disappear. A blanket of cold, white, soft snow is an immediate spur for a dog to go exploring and brings added excitement to retrieving a bone.

A dog's natural desire to dig in snow has been put to good use after mountain avalanches. Many a climber lost in the Swiss Alps has been saved by a rescue dog's acute sense of smell and determined digging.

The dog's natural retrieving instinct originated in its ancestral past when food was brought back to the den. Even animals which have lost some of this instinct quickly learn to respond to a thrown stick and the command 'fetch'.

Sometimes an excited dog races around with its prize in its mouth and may need patient coaxing to get it back so the game can continue. Some dogs will even tease their owners by offering the stick or ball and then snatching it away at the last moment. Throwing and fetching games are the best way for dogs to get plenty of exercise without their owners succumbing to fatigue!

Dogs usually remain playful well into adulthood and ball games are an enduring favourite with most of them. A dog will often initiate the fun, typically by placing a ball between its front paws and looking up with an expectant grin and happy thump of the tail.

Dogs also enjoy playing on their own. They will nose a ball up and down, round and round, until they eventually just run out of steam.

Some breeds of dog are particularly intelligent and can be trained to a high degree. The sight of a police dog displaying its skills, a guide dog leading its blind owner or a Border Collie herding unwilling sheep into pens is awe-inspiring to the average dog owner, whose commands may sometimes fall on very deaf ears.

An obedient dog is a credit to his or her owner and a pleasure to be with. Teaching your dog to sit, lie still and respond immediately when called is very important. Not only does it make your pet socially acceptable, it could even, in some circumstances, save his or her life.

T he Dobermann Pinscher was created in the
1890s by the German Louis Dobermann, by
crossing Rottweilers, German Pinschers and
Vorsthundes. A handsome, powerful dog with a
smooth glossy coat, it combines agility with speed
and a keen intelligence. It is primarily a working
dog and, under the control of an expert handler, is
capable of being an invaluable companion.

Dobermanns also have a protective instinct and
very quick reactions. They are employed
extensively as guard dogs and police dogs, for
which they undergo rigorous training. In this
capacity they may be used for chasing suspects,
sniffing out drugs and explosives, searching for
missing persons and riot control. A dog is especially
useful at night as its sharp senses, including
eyesight, are not handicapped by the dark.

earning to work with a handler as part of a team is essential to the training of dogs such as Dobermanns. They must be fit enough to scale high walls, find their way over or around obstacles, and swim considerable distances. They must not lose their nerve under gunfire. They must be able to mingle with the general public. Nervous and over-aggressive animals are not accepted for training as they tend to bite.

Lap dogs are small, docile and usually among the most pampered and privileged of pets. Pretty toy breeds like the Japanese Chin and Toy Spaniel are very popular. Other, more commonly seen, lap dogs include the long-haired Chihuahuas, Yorkshire Terriers and that earliest of toy breeds, the Maltese, which was known to the Ancient Greeks.

The exotic Papillon was a great favourite of the French court. It owes its name to the large fringed ears which sprout from its head like butterfly wings.

The lap-dog cult reached its height in China in 1820, with dogs tiny enough to be carried in the sleeves of dresses.

Lap dogs are usually well groomed and cared for, in order to enhance their attractive feature – perhaps a particularly long or glossy coat or unusual markings. Elaborate accessories are available, including bright ribbons (for long-haired breeds to keep the hair out of their eyes), jerseys, leggings and even rainhats.

<u>THE DOG AS A SPECIES</u>

Aglossy coat makes for a beautiful dog and is also an indication of good health. The distinctive black or liver-coloured dappling on the white fur of the Dalmatian has earned it the nickname 'the plum pudding dog'. Dalmatians were once used as a smart accessory to a horse and carriage; their speed and endurance enabled them to run beside the carriages for long distances. Nowadays they are popular for their amiable natures and comparative lack of 'doggy' smell. In contrast to the short coat of the Dalmatian, the Lhasa Apso's extraordinarily long hair makes grooming an essential feature of its care.

The Irish Water Spaniel is a handsome, powerful dog which is not commonly seen today. It was first used as a gun dog and is still employed for hunting wildfowl in marshes and lakes. Its densely curled coat is oily, making it water-resistant. However, although the richly coloured coat is ideal for a watery environment, it can cause problems on land – leaves, twigs and brambles are easily ensnared in the compact curls and it takes time and patience to extricate them.

The coat of the Old English Sheepdog has sometimes been combed and spun, then woven to make clothes. Once used as sheepdogs, highly regarded for their stamina, these 'Bob-tails' are no longer seen as working dogs.

The small, graceful Chinese Crested Dog is a striking example of a hairless breed. There seems to be no environmental or climatic reason for its hairlessness. Unless protected, the Chinese Crested is vulnerable to extremes of both heat and cold.

The size and shape of a dog's head differs enormously according to its breed. The Saluki has a notably streamlined narrow head, set on an elongated, supple neck which enhances the animal's graceful appearance. These dogs were originally used for catching gazelles in the Arabian deserts so they were bred for speed. Other breeds with long heads include the Afghan Hound, the Borzoi, the Scottish Deerhound and the Greyhound.

The massive head of the Bulldog breed is an example of the broad, square type. Bulldogs were used for bull-baiting as long ago as 1209, and a powerful bite was the main characteristic required. Nearly all the Oriental toy breeds are snub-nosed and flat-faced. The Pekingese is a classic specimen, as are the Japanese Chin and the Pug.

The Bull Terrier's head is particularly striking. It is long, egg-shaped, devoid of facial contours and set with tiny, triangular, obliquely slanting eyes.

The varying shape of dogs' ears is a result of domestication and breeding for appearance. Among wild dogs, from which all canines are descended, floppy ears are exclusively a feature of puppyhood and the ears become pricked as the animal approaches maturity. Some breeds, for example Alsatians, still have this characteristic, while the long, drooping ears of the Bedlington Terrier and the Porcelaine are a complete contrast, brought about by human intervention.

A dog's ears, particularly if erect, are an eloquent indicator of how it feels. Held flat against the head, they show submission or fear. Slightly lowered, they can demonstrate happy expectation of a pat on the head. Pricked, they indicate alertness and also aggression. The American Staffordshire Terrier is a descendant of the Staffordshire Bull Terrier; unlike its American counterpart, the latter has ears folded at the top.

The familiar saying that a dog's bark is worse than its bite is generally true, but most of us still find a barking dog threatening. Aggression, however, is expressed by growling and snarling and an all-out attack is almost always silent.

With the exception of the Basenji, which can only howl, dogs bark to sound a warning, to encourage their owners to feed them or take them for a walk, or to impress other animals with their fearlessness! The tone of a bark soon renders a dog's meaning clear to humans, whether it is excited, frightened, angry or unhappy.

A healthy canine mouth is pink and wet, with white, shining teeth. Puppies use their tongues to explore their environment and taste is as vital a canine sense as sight and smell. Licking is both an expression of affection and a means of grooming. In the wild, licking is part of dogs' greeting ritual.

Milk teeth appear around three to five weeks and the first adult teeth at about four months. Nowadays people tend to take more care of their pets' teeth. When a valuable police or guard dog loses a tooth, it can be replaced by a false steel one.

A dog's sense of smell is far superior to that of humans. Its nose contains 220 million smell-sensitive cells compared to our paltry five million. Some scientists claim that dogs' scent detection is 100 times greater than ours, others have put the figure as high as a million. In one test, six men briefly held a pebble before throwing it as far as they could. After a brief sniff of one man's hand, the dog used in the test was able to locate and retrieve his exact pebble.

The dog's olfactory acuteness has been put to many uses, including hunting truffles, routing out drugs and, of course, tracking down criminals. Sweat, particularly from human feet, is especially easy for a tracker dog to pick up. Of all dogs the Bloodhound is the most famous and probably the best at scent detection. It can follow a four-day-old trail for up to 100 miles without losing it.

CANINE CHARACTERISTICS

Digging is one of the most basic canine instincts, and most dogs, when given a bone, will attempt to bury it. This characteristic has been intensified in some breeds such as Lakeland and Fox Terriers, which have been bred for the purpose of digging foxes out of their dens. It's not unusual to see a dog digging apparently just for pleasure, forepaws working energetically, earth flying past its ears. Snow is delightfully easy to dig by contrast, although help from a human might be needed to remove packed ice from between the pawpads.

Water attracts many dogs and gun dogs in particular are good swimmers. Swimming will give a dog more exercise than an equivalent period of running and a stick thrown repeatedly into a pond will save a dog-owner many miles of walking. Breeds such as the Irish Water Spaniel and the Labrador are natural water dogs and will heartily relish a vigorous swim.

Dogs can make good sailors, soon adapting to the restrictions a boat imposes and its rocking motion. In fact, it's not unusual for a seafarer to choose a dog as a shipmate on a long haul. An intelligent mongrel called Mutley had a particular aptitude for ocean life and became his owner's scuba diving companion in California in 1983, wearing an especially adapted diving suit.

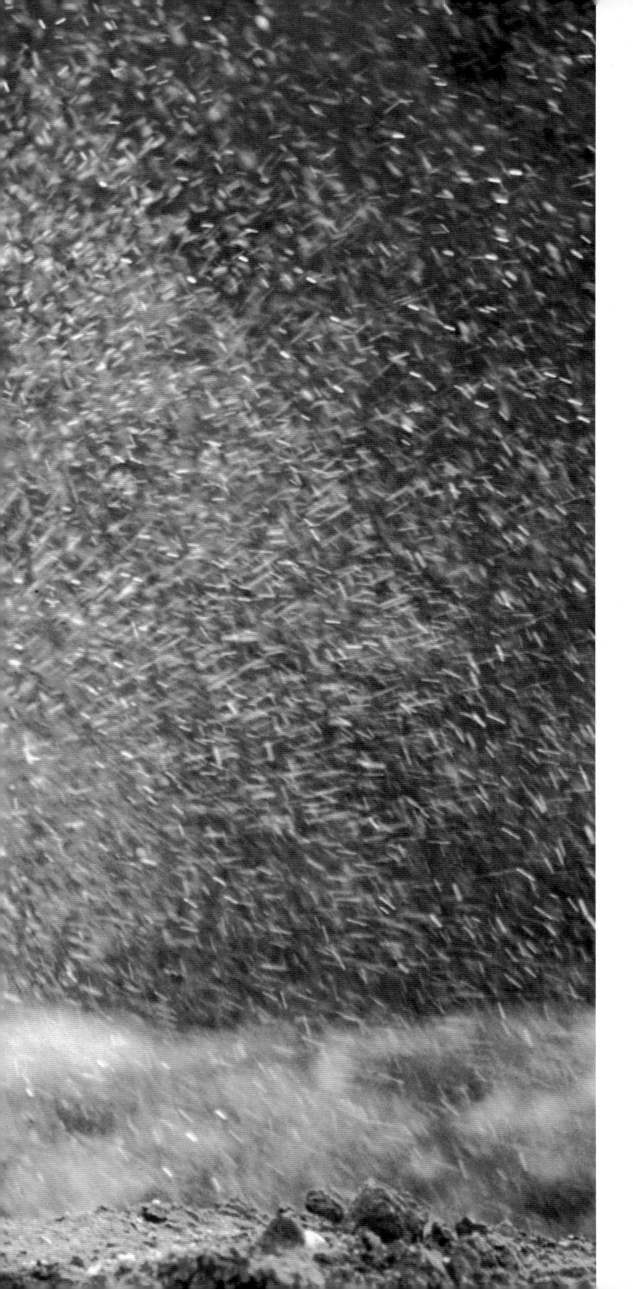

The sight of a dog enjoying a frolic in the sea is a familiar one. Most dogs love water and some of them even make a beeline for every muddy puddle they see. Carefully groomed pets emerge dripping and bedraggled, liberally dousing everything in their vicinity in the vigorous shaking that follows. Dogs appear to relish the shaking afterwards almost as much as playing in the water. Seasoned dog owners know to take hasty action to avoid their pet as it reaches dry land.

Strong, muscular and agile dogs are generally the best all-round athletes. A good example is the German Shepherd, which combines speed with an excellent high and long jumping ability. During the intensive training given to those dogs selected for police work, it learns to clear high walls, fences, gates and leap across ravines and wide, gaping ditches.

S ome members of the hound group are bred for stamina, while others are bred for speed. Foxhounds and Beagles run comparatively slowly, and can only catch a fox or hare when it tires after a long chase. Afghans, Salukis, Deerhounds, Borzois and Greyhounds were developed for coursing, where the hounds overtake prey such as gazelles and hares by virtue of sheer speed.

Of all great canine runners, Greyhounds are the most renowned. Originally bred to hunt in the desert, they relied on sight and exceptional speed to catch their prey. Ballyregan Bob, retired in 1987, is the fastest greyhound in history, running a record 7000 yards in under 40 seconds. Now a valuable stud, he is treated like a king and has two security guards keeping a 24-hour watch over his luxurious, well-kept kennel.

S ome dogs are incorrigibly greedy, soon
skilfully learning to thieve biscuits or titbits
from the kitchen table. Others, despite being
adequately fed, persist in rummaging through
dustbins for leftovers. Particularly wily curs visit
unsuspecting neighbours for extra food.

G nawing bones is very good for dogs' teeth; the marrow provides essential nutrients such as calcium and phosphorus which are lacking in meat. A constant supply of fresh water is essential for a dog, although some seem to prefer brackish pond water or muddy puddles.

Dogs often seem to spend much of the day dozing, and many also demand to share their owner's bed at night. Puppies sleep a lot more than adult dogs. Like all carnivores, dogs need to sleep after a meal to digest efficiently.

A bitch's pregnancy lasts nine weeks. Shortly before birth, she will make frantic digging movements on the floor of her chosen whelping area and, if she has a whelping box, will sometimes tear up rags or newspapers that have been placed in or near it. When all the puppies have been safely delivered and cleaned, the new mother has a well-earned rest while they take their first feed. The puppies are born blind, deaf and very vulnerable. The average size of a litter is five, although rare cases of more than 20 pups have been recorded.

At three weeks the first signs of tail-wagging and barking appear, and by now all breeds can see. Recent studies have shown that puppies are far more receptive to learning in their first few weeks than in later life. Three to nine weeks is the time when they are most responsive t their social environment.

The 'juvenile phase' begins at about 12 weeks. This is an exciting time when the dog's personality and characteristics really begin to emerge and training can be undertaken in earnest. The domestic pup also adapts socially at this age. In the wild, this is the age when the dog would start exploring its surroundings, joining the rest of the pack on hunts to learn its adult skills by following the example of the other dogs.

Certain characteristics in types of dogs may be strengthened by selective breeding. Man has always bred dogs to suit his own purposes, and in the process different breeds have evolved their own distinct features. In the past, dogs were bred for maximum efficiency in the job they were required to do. Since owning and exhibiting a pedigree animal has become a status symbol, however, the whole emphasis has altered radically. Nowadays dogs are often chosen simply because their physical appearance is appealing.

To conform to the rigidly imposed standards of accepted canine beauty, features such as short legs, very long bodies, flattened faces or diminutive size have been developed to the extreme. The closer the blood ties, the higher the chances that mating animals will pass specific characteristics and markings to their offspring.

Dogs frequently make friendships with other animals and stories abound of special relationships which develop between them. In 1983 an orphaned otter was taken to an animal sanctuary in Scotland. Its chances of survival were minimal until it was adopted by the sanctuary's pet spaniel, Tangle. In 1987, while out sailing with its owner in the West Indies, a mongrel made friends with a dolphin. The two have met for a daily frolic ever since.

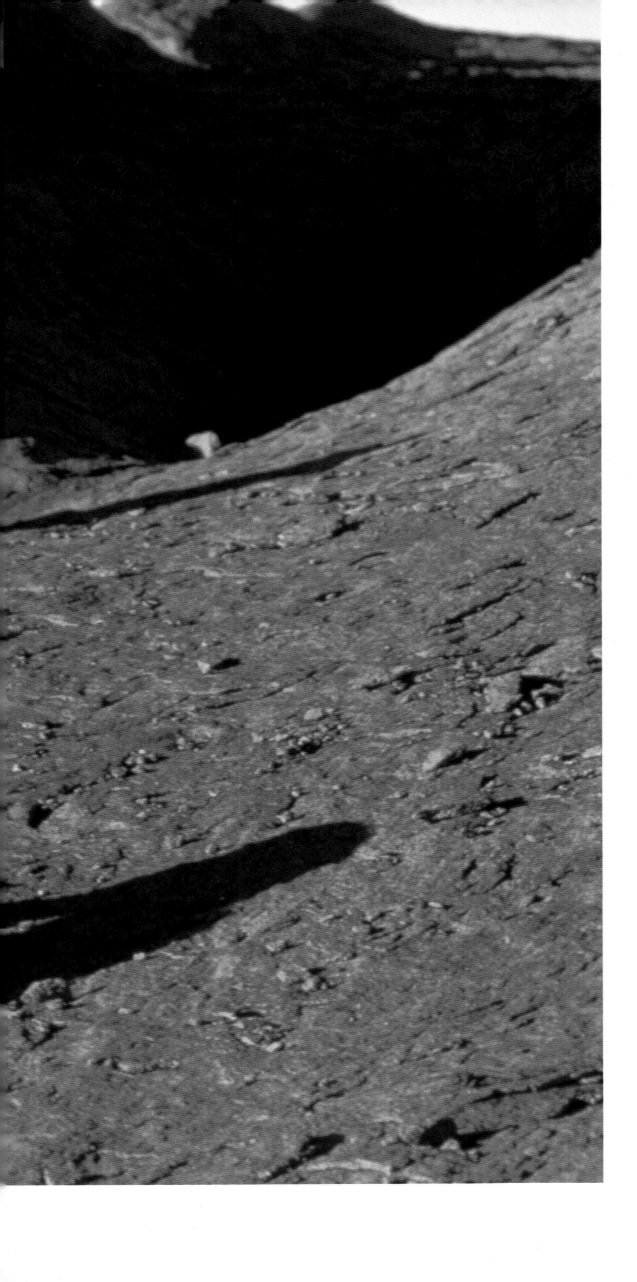

The Dingo is the native Australian wild dog. Endowed with cunning, courage and endurance, it hunts singly or in pairs, killing not only rabbits and rats, but attacking sheep, cattle and kangeroos.

Originally from South East Asia, the Dingo was brought to Australia by the Aborigines when they first settled the continent some 3000 years ago. It later mated with the domestic dogs that accompanied the British settlers and there are now very few pure Dingoes to be found. Dingo pups are still trained by Aborigines to hunt game.

DOGS AT WORK

Over the centuries humans have refined the dog's innate hunting instinct for maximum performance in the hunting field. The gun dog's acute sense of smell and ability to follow game into places inaccessible to its human companion has made it an invaluable and highly esteemed collaborator.

Some gun dogs flush out quarry, some retrieve, others point or set. A good gun dog is alert, enthusiastic but with a high degree of self-control. It must learn to wait patiently while its master shoots, restraining a natural urge to pursue and catch the prey itself.

Legend has it that when the Carthaginians arrived in Spain they were struck by the abundance of rabbits they found. Their word for rabbits was *span* and they therefore called the country *Hispania*, or Rabbitland. As a consequence, the dogs employed by the natives for hunting rabbits were called Spaniels.

Spaniels are particularly suited to rough shooting. Tough, tireless animals, they are natural hunters and retrievers and love water. The Spaniel group includes the Cocker, the English and Welsh Springer, the Irish Water and the Brittany Spaniels.

A Pointer is a specialized breed of gun dog whose job is to locate game in open country and then indicate its exact position to the hunters following. It does this by freezing in its tracks and adopting the famous 'pointing posture': head lowered and stretched forward, tail stiff and horizontal with one front paw held suspended mid-air. It is capable of holding this position for a long time with only a slight quivering of the tail to indicate its tense excitement. The dog relaxes when the hunter fires, causing the prey to break cover.

This distinctive behaviour originates in the dog's lupine ancestry. At the first scent of a quarry, leaders in a wolf pack stiffen into immobility and point rigidly in its direction.

Setters act in a somewhat similar way, the difference being that when they scent prey they point towards it from a sitting position.

The Labrador, one of the most popular gun dogs, arrived in Britain on the Newfoundland fishing boats that docked at Poole harbour in the mid-nineteenth century to sell their catch. It is a sturdily built, active dog with a distinctive, round, tapering tail and a keen intelligence. It didn't take long before the newcomer's excellent qualities were recognized by British sportsmen. The Labrador is courageous, fast and works well in water; its highly-developed scenting powers also make it a first-class game finder.

A dog's natural retrieving instincts date back to the ancestral wild state when food was carried back to the den. Gun dogs such as the Labrador are bred to enhance this instinct and are therefore easy to train for the hunting field. The black Labrador is more popular in the field, although the yellow is equally common in the show ring.

The Husky, also known as the Eskimo Dog, is famous for its strength, speed, intelligence and ability to endure the most austere conditions. For thousands of years human survival in the vast reaches of the frozen North was dependent on the Husky's efficiency.

Huskies strongly resemble the wolves from which they are descended and, because they are used in teams, their pack instinct remains strong. The head dog is very much the leader of each team and is always unharnessed and fed first to demonstrate its position of privilege to the other pack members.

In 1985 Nipper, the farm dog on Ansty Farm in Sussex, was awarded the animal world's VC for intelligence and courage. A fire in the largest barn spread with such devastating ferocity that only Nipper refused to abandon attempts to rescue the 300 assorted animals trapped inside. In spite of the smoke and flames he repeatedly ventured back into the barn to shepherd the terrified creatures to safety.

Pedigree or mongrel, farm dogs are an integral part of country life. They help farmers round up stock, keep down vermin and act as alert, responsible watchdogs.

The Border Collie is a common sight in sheep farming areas. These sheepdogs vary somewhat in appearance, some being the classic black and white long-coated collie, others having brindle, quite short fur. On hill farms, shepherding would be quite impossible without them.

A 'good eye' is essential in a sheepdog. This means that the dog is able to fix the sheep with such an intimidating stare that they will stay nervously where the dog wants. Sharp vision is vital, too, so that the dog can spot sheep which may be scattered far on the mountainside.

Although the St Bernard was probably introduced into Switzerland by invading Roman armies, it wasn't until the mid-seventeenth century that the monks of the Hospice du Grand St Bernard, high in the Swiss Alps, started breeding them as rescue dogs. The St Bernard possesses an astonishing sense of direction and is said to have a psychic awareness of impending disasters such as snowstorms and avalanches. Apparently it is also able to tell if a body buried under the snow is still alive or not.

Barry was the most famous of these dogs – indeed, such was his renown that for more than a century St Bernards were known as 'Barry dogs'. He worked at the Hospice from 1800 to 1812 and is claimed to have saved more than 40 lives.

ACKNOWLEDGEMENTS

All Sports/Grey Mortimore 54-5; Animal Photography/Sally Anne Thompson 6, 10, 13, 23 top, 24, 28, 30-1, 33, 34, 37, 40-1, 43, 44, 46-7, 52-3, 67, 74-5, 90-1, /R. Willbie 8-9, 14-15, 15, 19, 23 bottom, 35, 36 top, 42, 80-1, 82; Ardea/Jean-Paul Ferrero 27, 52; Marc Henrie 20-1, 26, 32, 58-9, 59, 78-9, 84-5, 92-3; Octopus Publishing Group Ltd/John Moss 18 inset/Peter Loughran 38; Spectrum Colour Library 16-17, 22, 44-5, 55 (inset), 60-1, 62-3, 68-9, 88-9; ZEFA Picture Library (UK) 1, 2, 5, 8, 11, 12-3, 14, 18-19, 24-5, 29, 36 bottom, 38-9, 41, 48-9, 50-1, 54, 56, 56-7, 63, 64-5, 66, 70-1, 72-3, 74, 76-7, 83, 86-7, 89 top, 94, 95.